The
Collected Works
of
Samuel Beckett

Other Works By Samuel Beckett
Published By Grove Press

Cascando and Other Short Dramatic Pieces
Film
Endgame
Happy Days
How It Is
Krapp's Last Tape and Other Dramatic Pieces
Murphy
Poems in English
Proust
Stories & Texts for Nothing
Molloy
Malone Dies
The Unnamable
Waiting for Godot
Watt

FILM

by Samuel Beckett

Complete scenario / Illustrations / Production shots

with an essay
On Directing *Film* by Alan Schneider

Grove Press, Inc., New York

Acknowledgments
Picture editor: David Woods   Book design: Kay Susmann

Beckett in room set.

Contents

Film (script with illustrations) / 9
Credits and Awards / 55
Notes on the Script by Samuel Beckett / 57
On Directing *Film* by Alan Schneider / 63
    (with production shots)

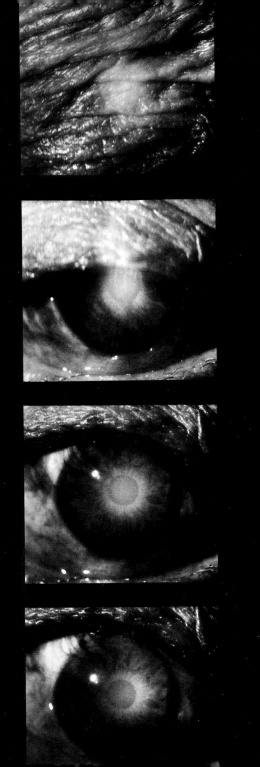

This is the original project for *Film*. No attempt has been made to bring it into line with the finished work. The one considerable departure from what was imagined concerns the opening sequence in the street. This was first shot as given, then replaced by a simplified version in which only the indispensable couple is retained. For the rest the shooting followed closely the indications of the script.

The film is divided into three parts. 1. The street (about eight minutes). 2. The stairs (about five minutes). 3. The room (about 17 minutes).

General

Esse est percipi.

All extraneous perception suppressed, animal, human, divine, self-perception maintains in being.

Search of non-being in flight from extraneous perception breaking down in inescapability of self-perception.

No truth value attaches to above, regarded as of merely structural and dramatic convenience.

In order to be figured in this situation the protagonist is sundered into object (O) and eye (E), the former in flight, the latter in pursuit.

It will not be clear until the end of film that pursuing perceiver is not extraneous, but self.

Until end of film O is perceived by E from behind and at an angle not exceeding 45°. Convention: O enters *percipi*=experiences anguish of perceivedness, only when this angle is exceeded.

E is therefore at pains, throughout pursuit, to keep within this "angle of immunity" and only exceeds it (1) inadvertently at beginning of part one when he first sights O, (2) inadvertently at beginning of part two when he. follows O into vestibule and (3) deliberately at end of part three when O is cornered. In first two cases he hastily reduces angle.

Throughout first two parts all perception is E's. E is the camera. But in third part there is O's perception of room and contents and at the same time E's continued perception of O. This poses a problem of images which I cannot solve without technical help. See below, note 8.

The film is entirely silent except for the "ssh!" in part one.

Climate of film comic and unreal. O should invite laughter throughout by his way of moving. Unreality of street scene (see notes to this section).

Outline

1. The street

Dead straight. No sidestreets or intersections. Period: about 1929. Early summer morning. Small factory district. Moderate animation of workers going unhurriedly to work. All going in same direction and all in couples. No automobiles. Two bicycles ridden by men with girl passengers (on crossbar). One cab, cantering nag, driver standing brandishing whip. All persons in opening scene to be shown in some way perceiving—one another, an object, a shop window, a poster, etc., i.e., all contentedly in *percipere* and *percipi*. First view of above is by E motionless and searching with his eyes for O. He may be supposed at street edge of wide (four yards) sidewalk. O finally comes into view hastening blindly along sidewalk, hugging the wall on his left, in opposite direction to all the others. Long dark overcoat (whereas all others in light summer dress) with collar up, hat pulled down over eyes, briefcase in left hand, right hand shielding exposed side of face. He storms along in comic foundered precipitancy. E's searching eye, turning left from street to sidewalk, picks him up at an angle exceeding that of immunity (O's unperceivedness according to convention) (1). O, entering perceivedness, reacts (after just sufficient onward movement for his gait to be established) by halting and cringing aside towards wall. E immediately draws back to close the angle (2) and O, re-

12

leased from perceivedness, hurries on. E lets him get about ten yards ahead and then starts after him (3). Street elements from now on incidental (except for episode of couple) in the sense that only registered in so far as they happen to enter field of pursuing eye fixed on O.

Episode of couple (4). In his blind haste O jostles an elderly couple of shabby genteel aspect, standing on sidewalk, peering together at a newspaper. They should be discovered by E a few yards before collision. The woman is holding a pet monkey under her left arm. E follows O an

instant as he hastens blindly on,* then registers couple recovering from shock, comes up with them, passes them slightly and halts to observe them (5). Having recovered they turn and look after O, the woman raising a *lorgnon* to her eyes, the man taking off his pince-nez fastened to

*At this point O's distorted vision is displayed cinematically. A brief, handheld shot (compatible with his haste) of first the man, then the woman (above) is shown; their images are blurred through a lens-gauze. (*Picture Ed.*)

his coat by a ribbon. They then look at each other, she lowering her *lorgnon*, he resuming his pince-nez. He opens his mouth to vituperate. She checks him with a gesture and soft "sssh!" He turns again, taking off his pince-nez, to look after O. She feels the gaze of E upon them and turns, raising her *lorgnon*, to look at him. She nudges her companion who turns back towards her, resuming his pince-nez, follows direction of her gaze and, taking off his pince-nez, looks at E. As they both stare at E the expression gradually comes over their faces which will be that of the flower-woman in the stairs scene and that of O at the end of film, an expression only to be described as corresponding to an agony of perceivedness. Indifference of monkey, looking up into face of its mistress. They close their eyes, she lowering her *lorgnon*, and hasten away in direction of all the others, i.e., that opposed to O and E (6).

E turns back towards O by now far ahead and out of sight. Immediate acceleration of E in pursuit (blurred transit of encountered elements). O comes into view, grows rapidly larger until E settles down behind him at same angle and remove as before. O disappears suddenly through open housedoor on his left. Immediate acceleration of E who comes up with O in vestibule at foot of stairs. *

2. The stairs

Vestibule about four yards square with stairs at inner righthand angle. Relation of streetdoor to stairs such that E's first perception of O (E near door, O motionless at foot of stairs, right hand on banister, body shaken by panting) is from an angle a little exceeding that of immunity. O, entering perceivedness (according to convention), transfers right hand from banister to exposed side of face and cringes aside towards wall on his left. E immediately draws back to close the angle and O, released, resumes his pose at foot of stairs, hand on banister. O mounts a few steps (E remaining near door), raises head, listens, redescends hastily backwards and crouches down in angle of stairs and wall on his right, invisible to one descending (7). E registers him there, then transfers to stairs.

18

A frail old woman appears on bottom landing. She carries a tray of flowers slung from her neck by a strap. She descends slowly, with fumbling feet, one hand steadying the tray, the other holding the banister.*Absorbed by difficulty of descent she does not become aware of E until she is quite down and making for the door. She halts and looks full at E. Gradually same expression as that of couple in street. She closes her eyes, then sinks to the ground and lies with face in scattered flowers. E lingers on this a moment, then transfers to where O last registered. He is no longer there, but hastening up the stairs. E transfers to stairs and picks up O as he reaches first landing. Bound forwards and up of E who overtakes O on second flight and is literally at his heels when he reaches second landing

*E's and O's views respectively (left to right) of the old flower-woman's hand. (*Picture Ed.*)

and opens with key door of room. They enter room together, E turning with O as he turns to lock the door behind him.

3. The room

Here we assume problem of dual perception solved and enter O's perception (8). E must so manoeuvre throughout what follows, until investment proper, that O is always seen from behind, at most convenient remove, and from an angle never exceeding that of immunity, i.e., preserved from perceivedness.

Small barely furnished room (9). Side by side on floor a large cat and small dog. Unreal quality. Motionless till ejected. Cat bigger than dog. On a table against wall a parrot in a cage and a goldfish in a bowl. This room sequence falls into three parts.

1. Preparation of room (occlusion of windows and mirror, ejection of dog and cat, destruction of print, occlusion of parrot and goldfish).

2. Period in rocking-chair. Inspection and destruction of photographs.

3. Final investment of O by E and dénouement.

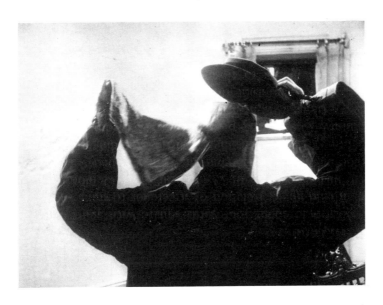

1. O stands near door with case in hand and takes in room. Succession of images: dog and cat, side by side, staring at him; mirror; window; couch with rug; dog and cat staring at him; parrot and goldfish, parrot staring at him; rocking-chair; dog and cat staring at him. He sets down

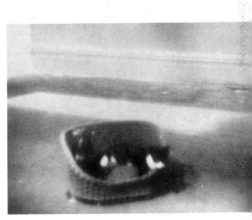

case, approaches window from side and draws curtain. He turns towards dog and cat, still staring at him, then goes to couch and takes up rug. He turns towards dog and cat, still staring at him. Holding rug before him he approaches

mirror from side and covers it with rug. He turns towards parrot and goldfish, parrot still staring at him. He goes to rocking-chair, inspects it from front. Insistent image of curiously carved headrest (10). He turns towards dog and

*O turning the animals' faces away to avert their stare. (*Picture Ed.*)

cat still staring at him. He puts them out of room (11)*.
He takes up case and is moving towards chair when rug
falls from mirror. He drops case, hastens to wall between couch and mirror, follows walls past window,

*After a sequence when first one animal then the other runs back
into the room as O is ejecting the other. At last, when they are both
out, O gestures at the door. (*Picture Ed.*)

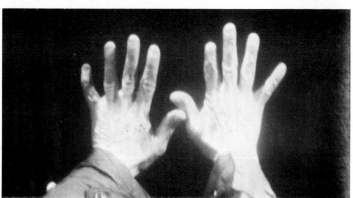

approaches mirror from side, picks up rug and, holding it
before him, covers mirror with it again. He returns to
case, picks it up, goes to chair, sits down and is opening
case when disturbed by print, pinned to wall before him, of

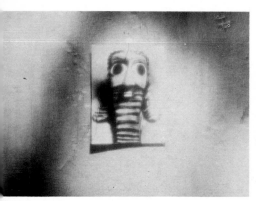 

the face of God the Father, the eyes staring at him severely. He sets down case on floor to his left, gets up and inspects print. Insistent image of wall, paper hanging off in strips (10). He tears print from wall, tears it in four,

throws down the pieces and grinds them underfoot. He turns back to chair, image again of its curious headrest, sits down, image again of tattered wall-paper, takes case on his knees, takes out a folder,* sets down case on floor to his

*To avert the "eyes" on the folder, O turns it 90°. (*Picture Ed.*)

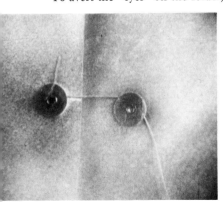

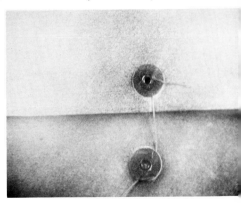

left and is opening folder when disturbed by parrot's eye. He lays folder on case, gets up, takes off overcoat, goes to parrot, close-up of parrot's eye, covers cage with coat, goes back to chair, image again of headrest, sits down, image

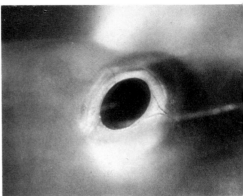

again of tattered wall-paper, takes up folder and is opening it when disturbed by fish's eye. He lays folder on case, gets up, goes to fish, close-up of fish's eye, extends coat to cover bowl as well as cage, goes back to chair, image again

of headrest, sits down, image again of wall, takes up folder, takes off hat and lays it on case to his left. Scant hair or bald, to facilitate identification of narrow black elastic encircling head.

When O sits up and back his head is framed in headrest which is a narrower extension of backrest. Throughout scene of inspection and destruction of photographs E may be supposed immediately behind chair looking down over O's left shoulder (12).

2. O opens folder, takes from it a packet of photographs

(13), lays folder on case and begins to inspect photographs. He inspects them in order 1 to 7. When he has finished with 1 he lays it on his knees, inspects 2, lays it on top of 1, and so on, so that when he has finished inspecting them all 1 will be at the bottom of the pile and 7—or rather 6, for he does not lay down 7—at the top. He gives about six seconds each to 1–4, about twice as long to 5 and 6 (trembling hands). Looking at 6 he touches with forefinger little girl's face. After six seconds of 7 he tears it in four and drops pieces on floor on his left. He takes up 6 from top of

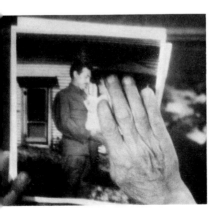

pile on his knees, looks at it again for about three seconds, tears it in four and drops pieces on floor to his left. So on for the others, looking at each again for about three seconds before tearing it up. 1 must be on tougher mount for he

has difficulty in tearing it across. Straining hands. He finally succeeds, drops pieces on floor and sits, rocking slightly, hands holding armrests (14).

3. Investment proper. Perception from now on, if dual

perception feasible, E's alone, except perception of E by O at end. E moves a little back (image of headrest from back), then starts circling to his left, approaches maximum angle and halts. From this open angle, beyond which he will enter *percipi*, O can be seen beginning to doze off. His visible hand relaxes on armrest, his head nods and falls forward, the rock approaches stillness. E advances, opening angle beyond limit of immunity, his gaze pierces the light sleep and O starts awake. The start revives the rock, immediately arrested by foot to floor. Tension of hand on armrest. Turning his head to right, O cringes away from perceivedness. E draws back to reduce the angle and after a moment, reassured, O turns back front and resumes his pose. The rock resumes, dies down slowly as O dozes off again. E now begins a much wider encirclement. Images of curtained window, walls, and shrouded mirror to indicate his path and that he is not yet looking at O. Then brief image of O seen by E from well beyond the angle of immunity, i.e., from near the table with shrouded bowl and cage. O is now seen to be fast asleep, his head sunk on his chest and his hands, fallen from the armrests, limply dangling. E resumes his cautious approach. Images of shrouded bowl and cage and tattered wall adjoining, with same indication as before. Halt and brief image, not far short of full-face, of O still fast asleep. E advances last few yards along tattered wall and halts directly in front of O. Long image of O, full-face, against ground of headrest, sleeping. E's gaze pierces the

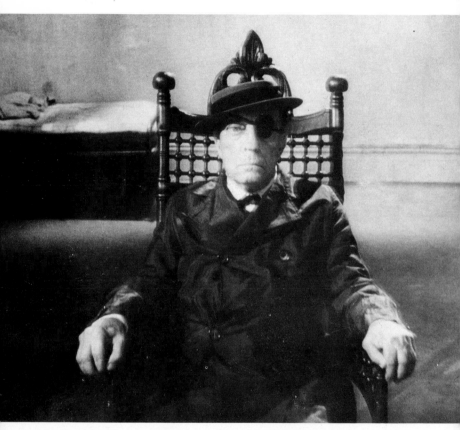

sleep, O starts awake, stares up at E. Patch over O's left
eye now seen for first time. Rock revived by start, stilled at

once by foot to ground. Hands clutch armrests. O half starts from chair, then stiffens, staring up at E.

Gradually that look.

Cut to E, of whom this very first image (face only, against ground of tattered wall). It is O's face (with patch) but with very different expression, impossible to describe, neither severity nor benignity, but rather acute *intentness*. A big nail is visible near left temple (patch side). Long image of the unblinking gaze. Cut back to O, still half risen, staring up, with that look. O closes his eyes and falls back in chair, starting off rock. He covers his face with his hands. Image of O rocking, his head in his hands but not yet bowed.

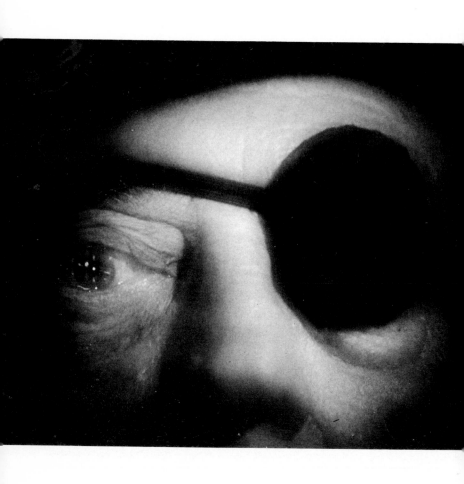

Cut back to E. As before. Cut back to

O. He sits, bowed forward, his head in his hands, gently rocking. Hold it as the rocking dies down.

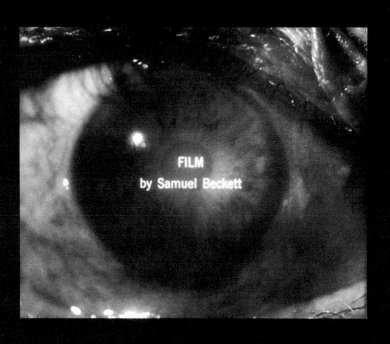

FILM
by Samuel Beckett

Credits and Awards

FILM

22 minutes
Black and white
Shot in 35mm
Released in 35mm and 16mm

Director:	Alan Schneider
Scenario:	Samuel Beckett
Cinematographer:	Boris Kaufman
Camera Operator:	Joe Coffey
Editor:	Sidney Meyers
Cast:	Buster Keaton

No dialogue   Aspect Ratio normal

Produced by Evergreen Theatre, Inc.

Festivals

Venice Film Festival, 1965
Diploma di Merito

New York Film Festival, 1965

London Film Festival, 1965
An Outstanding Film of the Year

Oberhausen Film Festival, 1966
Preis der Kurtzfilmtage

Tours Film Festival, 1966
Prix Spécial du Jury

Sidney Film Festival, 1966

Kraków Film Festival, 1966

Notes

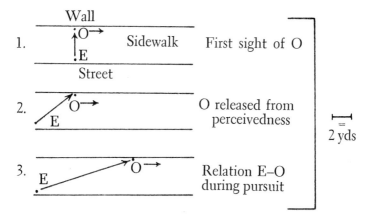

1. First sight of O

2. O released from perceivedness

3. Relation E–O during pursuit

⊢—⊣ = 2 yds

4. The purpose of this episode, undefendable except as a dramatic convenience, is to suggest as soon as possible unbearable quality of E's scrutiny. Reinforced by episode of flower-woman in stairs sequence.

5. ⊢—⊣ = 2 yds

6. Expression of this episode, like that of animals' ejection in part three, should be as precisely stylized as possible. The purpose of the monkey, either unaware of E or indifferent to him, is to anticipate behaviour of animals in part three, attentive to O exclusively.

7. Suggestion for vestibule with (1) O in *percipi* (2) released (3) hiding from flower-woman. Note that even when E exceeds angle of immunity O's face never really seen because of immediate turn aside and (here) hand to shield face.

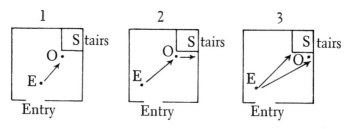

8. Up till now the perceptions of O, hastening *blindly* to illusory sanctuary, have been neglected and must in fact have been negligible. But in the room, until he falls asleep and the investment begins, they must be recorded. And at the same time E's perceiving of O must continue to be given. E is concerned only with O, not with the room, or only incidentally with the room in so far as its elements happen to enter the field of his gaze fastened on O. We see O in the room thanks to E's perceiving and the room itself thanks to O's perceiving. In other words this room sequence, up to the moment of O's falling asleep, is composed of two independent sets of images. I feel that any attempt to express them in simultaneity (composite images, double frame, superimposition, etc.) must prove unsatisfactory. The presentation in a single image of O's perception of the print, for example, and E's perception of O perceiving it—no doubt feasible technically—would per-

haps make impossible for the spectator a clear apprehension of either. The solution might be in a succession of images of different *quality*, corresponding on the one hand to E's perception of O and on the other to O's perception of the room. This difference of quality might perhaps be sought in different degrees of development, the passage from the one to the other being from greater to lesser and lesser to greater definition or luminosity. The dissimilarity, however

58

obtained, would have to be flagrant. Having been up till now exclusively in the E quality, we would suddenly pass, with O's first survey of the room, into this different O quality. Then back to the E quality when O is shown moving to the window. And so on throughout the sequence, switching from the one to the other as required. Were this the solution adopted it might be desirable to establish, by means of brief sequences, the O quality in parts one and two.

This seems to be the chief problem of the film, though I perhaps exaggerate its difficulty through technical ignorance.

9.

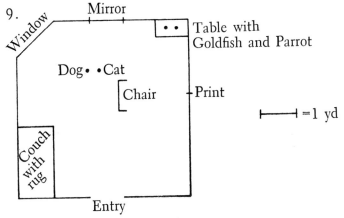

Suggestion for room.

This obviously cannot be O's room. It may be supposed it is his mother's room, which he has not visited for many years and is now to occupy momentarily, to look after the pets, until she comes out of hospital. This has no bearing on the film and need not be elucidated.

10. At close of film face E and face O can only be distinguished (1) by different expressions, (2) by fact of O looking up and E down and (3) by difference of ground

(for O headrest of chair, for E wall). Hence insistence on headrest and tattered wall.

11. Foolish suggestion for eviction of cat and dog. Also see note 6.

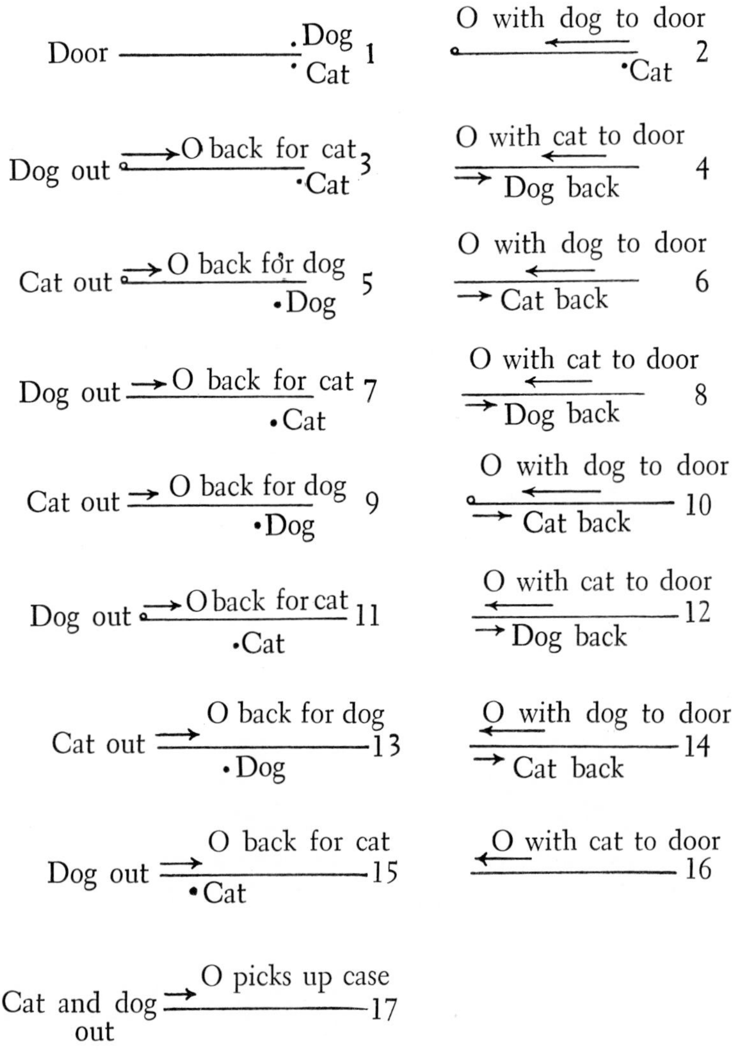

Door ————————— .Dog 1
                  · Cat

O with dog to door
←————————————
              ·Cat 2

Dog out ——→O back for cat 3
                    ·Cat

O with cat to door
←————————————
  → Dog back 4

Cat out ——→O back for dog 5
                  ·Dog

O with dog to door
←————————————
  → Cat back 6

Dog out —→O back for cat 7
                  ·Cat

O with cat to door
←————————————
  → Dog back 8

Cat out —→ O back for dog 9
                  ·Dog

O with dog to door
←————————————
  → Cat back 10

Dog out —→O back for cat 11
                  ·Cat

O with cat to door
←————————————
  → Dog back 12

Cat out —→ O back for dog 13
                · Dog

O with dog to door
←————————————
  → Cat back 14

Dog out —→ O back for cat 15
              ·Cat

O with cat to door
←———————————— 16

Cat and dog —→ O picks up case 17
  out

12. Chair from front during photo sequence.

13. Description of photographs.

1. Male infant. Six months. His mother holds him in her arms. Infant smiles front. Mother's big hands. Her severe eyes devouring him. Her big old-fashioned beflowered hat.

2. The same. Four years. On a veranda, dressed in loose nightshirt, kneeling on a cushion, attitude of prayer, hands clasped, head bowed, eyes closed. Half profile. Mother on chair beside him, big hands on knees, head bowed towards him, severe eyes, similar hat to 1.

3. The same. 15 years. Bareheaded. School blazer. Smiling. Teaching a dog to beg. Dog on its hind legs looking up at him.

4. The same. 20 years. Graduation day. Academic gown. Mortar-board under arm. On a platform, receiving scroll from Rector. Smiling. Section of public watching.

5. The same. 21 years. Bareheaded. Smiling. Small moustache. Arm round fiancée. A young man takes a snap of them.

6. The same. 25 years. Newly enlisted. Bareheaded. Uniform. Bigger moustache. Smiling. Holding a little girl in his arms. She looks into his face, exploring it with finger.

7. The same. 30 years. Looking over 40. Wearing hat and overcoat. Patch over left eye. Cleanshaven. Grim expression.

14. Profit by rocking-chair to emotionalize inspection, e.g., gentle steady rock for 1 to 4, rock stilled (foot to ground) after two seconds of 5, rock resumed between 5 and 6, rock stilled after two seconds of 6, rock resumed after 6 and for 7 as for 1–4.

On Directing *Film*

With every new wavelet of contemporary cinema turning directors, in effect, into authors, it took the surprising author of *Film*, playwright Samuel Beckett, to become, not too surprisingly, its real director. Not that I wasn't always around, red director's cap flying, riding the camera dolly, or telling Buster what to do. But, from original concept to final cut, it was the special vision and tone set by Sam which all of us were dedicated to putting on film—our intrepid producer, Barney Rosset; Boris Kaufman, our quiet painstaking director of photography; Joe Coffey, that great bearded sweating giant of a camera operator; Sidney Meyers, the most sensitive of editors; Burr Smidt, our friendly resourceful designer; and even, in his way, a baffled but most amenable Keaton. Sometimes we glimpsed that vision clearly. Sometimes we fought it. Sometimes, many times, I'm afraid, we tried to achieve it and failed. Once or twice, we may have transmuted it into something it wasn't; perhaps, as in Sam's generous words afterward, acquiring "a dimension and validity of its own that are worth far more than any merely efficient translation of intention." But, in the process, it was exactly that faithful translation of intention we were all after.

Film was a short film commissioned for Evergreen Theatre. The script appeared in the spring of 1963 as a fairly baffling when not downright inscrutable six-page outline. Along with pages of addenda in Sam's inimitable informal style: explanatory notes, a philosophical supplement, modest production suggestions, a series of hand-drawn diagrams. Involving, in cosmic detail, his principal characters, O and E, the question of "perceivedness," the angle of immunity, and the essential principle that *esse est percipi*: to be is to be perceived. All composed with loving care, humor, sadness, and Sam's ever-present compassionate understanding of man's essential frailty. I loved it even when

...aton on street location with Schneider (with bull horn).

Beckett, Seaver, Kaufman, Schneider and
Coffey on street location.

I wasn't completely sure what Sam meant. And I suddenly decided that my early academic training in physics and geometry was finally going to 'pay off in my directorial career.

Came then almost a year of preparation. Reading and rereading the "script," which, of course, had no dialogue (with the exception of that one whispered "sssh!"); asking Sam a thousand questions, largely by mail and eventually in person at his Montparnasse apartment; trying to visualize graphically and specifically the varied demands of those six tantalizing pages. Gradually, the mysteries and enigmas, common denominators of all new Beckett works, came into focus with fascinatingly simple clarity. The audacity of his concept—a highly disciplined use of two specific camera viewpoints—emerged from behind all the seeming ambiguities of the technical explanations. (After all, it was Sam who had written a play mastering the definitive use of a tape recorder even though he had never owned one.) I began to work out a tentative shooting script.

What was required was not merely a subjective camera and an objective camera, but actually two different "visions" of reality: one, that of the perceiving "eye" (E) constantly observing the object (the script was once titled *The Eye*), and one, that of the object (O) observing his environment. O was to possess varying degrees of awareness of being perceived by E and make varying attempts to escape from this perception (in addition to all other, or even imagined, perceptions). The story of this highly visual, if highly unusual, film was simply that O's attempt to remove all perception ultimately failed because he could not get rid of self-perception. At the end, we would see that $O = E$. Q.E.D.

What became immediately clear was that whenever the camera was O, it would, of course, not see or show any parts of O. Whenever the camera was E, it would always have to be more or less directly behind O, never actually seeing O's face from front until the very last shot of confrontation. What actor of star stature would be willing to play a part in which we would almost never see his face? Which cameraman of first rank would risk the danger to his reputation resulting from such a limited range of camera placement?

From the beginning, in keeping with Sam's feeling that the film should possess a slightly stylized comic reality akin to that of a silent movie, we thought in terms of Chaplin or Zero Mostel for O. Chaplin, as we expected, was totally inaccessible; Mostel, unavailable. We hit upon Jackie MacGowran, a favorite of both Beckett and me. Jackie is a delicious comedian and had been an inveterate performer of Beckett's plays in England and Ireland; he understood and felt with the material without an extra word of explanation. Luckily, Jackie had just been acclaimed in the small but juicy role of the Highwayman in *Tom Jones* so that he was suddenly "saleable." We acquired (not too easily) a cameraman and the beginnings of a staff. We also picked our shooting date and location: June of 1964, somewhere in Greenwich Village.

Best of all, we had finally persuaded Beckett to come to New York for the shooting, an objective which had not been reached for any of his previous productions. Sam didn't really want to come. New York, he assumed, would be too loud and too demanding, too many interviews and cocktail parties. He preferred the quiet of Paris and his country retreat at Ussy. But to work on this one, he would. June 6. (Original schedule.)

Then, in the usual fashion, things began to happen. The picture was far from conventional, but the events surrounding its preparation proved to be so. First, even before we got started, the budget went up. We lost our cameraman to some Hollywood epic. The people who owned the small New York studio where we were going to shoot our single interior, and who were going to be involved on a co-production basis, got cold feet. Jackie got a feature film which made his summer availability dangerously tight. I got increasingly nervous and kept asking for more preparation time (among other things, someone at the Guthrie Theatre had told me that any sequence with cats was impossible) although I knew that any delay meant we might wind up losing Jackie. And the budget kept going up.

With the rest of us suffering various degrees of panic, Sam reacted to all developments with characteristic resilience and understanding. During a transatlantic call one day (as I remember) he shattered our desperation over the sudden casting crisis by calmly suggesting Buster Keaton. Was Buster still alive and well? (He was.) How would he react to acting in Beckett material? (He'd been offered the part of Lucky in the original American *Godot* some years back, and had turned it down.) Would this turn out to be a Keaton film rather than a Beckett film? (Sam wasn't worrying about that.)

Off went the script to Keaton, followed a few days later by the director's first voyage to Hollywood—to woo Buster. It was a weird experience. Late one hot night, I arrived at Keaton's house, in a remote section of Los Angeles, to discover that I seemed to have interrupted a four-handed poker game. Apologizing, I was told that the poker game was imaginary (with long-since departed Irving Thalberg, Nicholas Schenk, and somebody else), had been going on since 1927, and Thalberg owed Keaton over two million dollars (imaginary, I hoped). We went on from there, when I suddenly realized that everything in the room harked back to circa 1927 or earlier. Keaton had read the script and was not sure what could be done to fix it up. His general attitude was that we were all, Beckett included,

67

nuts. But he needed the money, a handsome sum for less than three weeks' work, and would do it. Yes, he remembered the *Godot* business, but he didn't understand that one either.

Keaton made no effort to disguise his general bafflement. The script was not only unclear, he admitted, it wasn't funny. Here he suggested some special business with his walk, or perhaps that bit where he could keep sharpening a pencil and it would get smaller and smaller. I said that we didn't normally pad Beckett's material. Then he told me, confidentially, that he had made a lot of movies in his time and didn't see how this one could possibly play more than four minutes. He had timed it. Even if we stretched that cat and dog business, which wasn't too bad. He'd be glad—for a fee—to supply some ideas. From 1927.

On the way home I worried considerably about Keaton; but, like Everest, he was there and, with Sam's encouragement, we had to have him.

Our casting complete, we still needed a great photographer and an editor without too strong an ego. With time at a premium, we were fortunate enough to persuade Kaufman and Meyers that Beckett had not lost his mind in confining those camera angles so rigidly, nor was he willing to expand them. Sam arrived, late on July 10, for our first big weekend production conference (at Barney Rosset's poolside in Easthampton, just like Hollywood!) flying to Idlewild and then directly to the tip of Long Island in a privately hired plane which, to our horror, turned out to be hardly large enough to hold his long legs. For three days we talked, walked, and sat. (We also played tennis.) Sam explained the necessary camera positions and angles to all concerned (nor did he budge from his fundamental position in the face of some highly sophisticated arguments about the new-found flexibility and mobility of the film medium), and tried to explain the exact difference of in-

Beckett on street location with Barney Rosset.

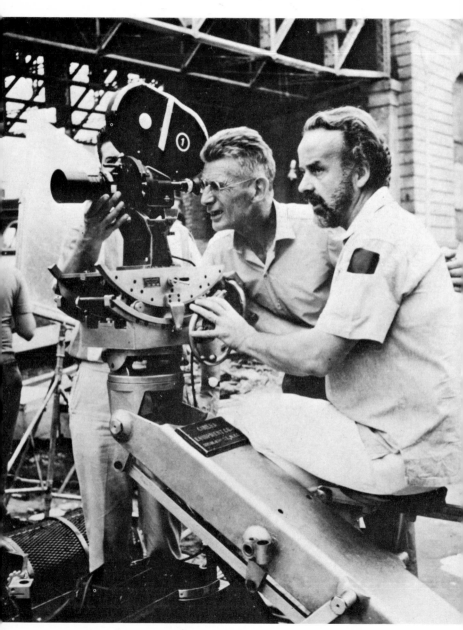

Beckett on street location with camera operator Joe Coffey.

tensity he wanted in the separate visions of O and E. The rough shooting script got revised into an exact shooting script, and I kept wishing I'd had one of Mr. Krapp's abandoned tape recorders around.

In New York, for a week, we continued to talk, walk, and also sit down occasionally. Sam decided that the city wasn't as bad as he had feared; he especially liked the Village, and managed a special pilgrimage to the Cherry Lane Theatre, home for so many of his plays. We scouted locations and eventually found one that fitted Sam's liking, although it turned out to be an about-to-be-knocked-apart wall way down in lower Manhattan rather than the ones we'd tentatively picked for his approval on Commerce Street or Minetta Lane. We were getting close.

Then came the meeting we'd waited for and worried about. A few days before shooting was to start, Keaton had arrived in Manhattan, for the first time in many years. I took him to be photographed and to pick out his costume and eye-patch, showed him the city and, ultimately, the author. That meeting of Beckett and Keaton, one afternoon in the latter's hotel suite, was one of those occasions which seem inevitable before they take place, impossible when they do, and unbelievable afterward. Sam had been expectantly awaiting Keaton's arrival; he had known and respected his work since the days of the old silent films. Keaton, knowing of Sam's standing as a playwright and novelist, was intrigued, but didn't really know what to make of a man like Beckett. When Sam and I arrived, Keaton was drinking a can of beer and watching a baseball game on TV; his wife was in the other room. The greetings were mild, slightly awkward somehow, without meaning to be. The two exchanged a few general words, most of them coming from Sam, then proceeded to sit there in silence while Keaton kept watching the game. I don't even think he offered us a beer. Not out of ill will; he just didn't think

71

of it. Or else maybe he thought that a man like Beckett didn't drink beer.

Now and then, Sam—or I—would try to say something to show some interest in Keaton, or just to keep the non-existent conversation going. It was no use. Keaton would answer in monosyllables and get right back to the Yankees —or was it the Mets?

"Did you have any questions about anything in the script, Buster?"

"No."

(Pause.)

"What did you think about the film when you first read it?"

"Well . . ."

(Long pause.)

And so on. It was harrowing. And hopeless. The silence became an interminable seventh-inning stretch.

They simply had nothing to say to each other, no worlds of any kind to share. And all of Sam's good will and my own flailing efforts to get something started failed to bring them together on any level.

It was a disaster.

Oh, yes, just before we left, Keaton made some comment about his old flattened-down Stetson being his trademark (perhaps Sam asked him), and mentioned that he'd brought several of them along in different colors to use in the film. (The script called for slightly different headgear.) While I was figuring out how to react to this choice between Scylla and Charybdis, Sam replied—to my surprised delight—that he didn't see why Buster couldn't wear his own hat in this one. And then proceeded to demonstrate how the handkerchief worn inside of it (to hide his face from E in that first sequence of running along the wall) might be more interesting than what was originally called for.

We didn't talk too much about Keaton that evening. Although I remember distinctly trying to recall, in as much detail as I could manage, the high points of his performances in *The Navigator* and *The General*.

On Monday morning, July 20, we traipsed down in Joe Coffey's ancient Morgan to just beneath the shadow of Brooklyn Bridge and began the shooting. My introduction to filmmaking. Much hoopla: lots of reporters, hordes of onlookers, Alain Resnais. The sequence was a tough one: light problems, traffic problems, actor problems (the most important two supporting actors in the morning's shooting managed to get delayed two hours crossing the George Washington Bridge), and camera problems (wobbling dollies, ill-matched swish pans, strobe effects creeping in—a strobe effect, I discovered, occurs when the background undulates on a pan shot). Beginning-director problems. I didn't even know there was such a thing as a strobe effect, so I went right on panning the extras up and down the street. There seemed to be thousands.

But I managed to get water on the pavement.

In retrospect, for example, while watching the rushes the next day, I wished we had not started with what really was a massive outdoor sequence. Too many things went wrong. The time went too fast. I didn't always know or even suspect what I was doing. But at the time things didn't seem all bad. The group shots, with which the picture started before Keaton came on, seemed, after many a slip, to be working reasonably well. Except for Boris, who kept looking sadly at the sun through a dark lens, everybody kept saying friendly things to me. There was a general feeling that we were making progress, though I kept having my doubts.

The one thing I was sure of was that Buster was turning out to be magnificent. He was totally professional: patient, unperturbable, relaxed, easy to tell something to, helpful, there. He must have been over seventy, but he never complained for a single moment when we asked him, for some reason or other, to run along that obstacle course of a wall over and over again in the broiling heat. Nor did he object when we kept adding obstacles that would have bothered a steeplechase expert. Or nag when something went wrong with something, which happened at least sixty percent of the time, or when we didn't do something the way he did it in 1927. He didn't even mention 1927 that day. He didn't smile either, but then he smiled rarely, off-screen or on.

I finally went home, drained, five pounds lighter, six years older, but relatively happy about movie-making. And radiant about our choice of Buster.

The second day provided different problems but was about as horrendous as the first. We were shooting in a hallway and up some stairs. There was no room for anything or anyone. The lights were inadequate. The camera couldn't move in the direction nor at the speed we wanted it to. We had to completely restage Keaton's main action in the sequence. Even then, something was wrong with the timing, and Sidney kept saying we should be shooting it differently. The hallway was packed with people, and I couldn't ever get where I wanted to be. It was hotter than a steam room. Everything took forever. We must have used up half of the budget on overtime, not to mention all of our energy and will power.

Worst of all, we saw the first day's rushes. I thought at first that they looked pretty good here and there, except for those two actors who had been late and had had to be dressed, made-up, rehearsed, and shot in too much of a hurry. (Of course, I was so convinced that there had been no film in the camera, or if some had gotten in by accident it probably had been improperly exposed, that any exposed film inevitably seemed to me of Academy Award caliber.)

74

Beckett, Schneider, Keaton on street location.

Extras on street location. Characters cut.

Everything looked completely different from the way it had while we were shooting it, the timing was so changed that I could not understand it at all, I cursed the jiggling dolly and the rough roadbed and Joe Coffey for telling me the shot was smooth—but there were possibilities, I thought.

I was the only one. Everyone else, from Sam to the producer, suffered glum despair. The lighting was gloomy throughout. The performances, except for Buster's, were terrible. The group scenes suffered so badly from that strobe effect that they were impossible to watch. In everyone's opinion, none of the scenes involving the other actors (except the tardy couple who were bad but bearable) was even remotely usable. And the budget would not permit our going down there again to do everything over. It was another disaster, a real one.

Again, it was Sam who saved the day, this time the night. Piercing through what was beginning to be an atmosphere of some rancor and bitterness, Sam proposed in a quiet voice the ultimate solution: eliminate the entire sequence. Start with Buster running along the wall (preceded by E's eye). That made great sense, he thought. He had never been sure all those people belonged in that opening anyway. They gave it and the film a different texture, opened up another world. Besides, even excluding that damned strobe effect—which was rapidly becoming the star of the picture—they weren't very good.

Sam was incredible. People always assumed him to be totally unyielding, made of granite; his photographs tended to make him look that way. Yet, when the chips were down, on specifics—here as well as on all the stage productions of his I had done—he was always yielding, completely understanding, and flexible. Not absolute but pragmatic. Far from blaming anything on the limitations and mistakes of those around him, he blamed his own material, himself. He had no recriminations for me or anyone else. He was even prepared to eliminate an important segment of his film. I was ready to quit, kill myself, cry, do it all over again on the sly, anything! In vain.

The next morning, and for three weeks, we shot in our one interior set up at the studio, small but adequate, on the upper West Side. That was a lot easier. And better. (Besides, the rushes of the hallway scene from the second day weren't too bad. The flower lady, Sam thought, was beautiful. So did I.) Most of the time I didn't even have to choose the camera's position or angle; we just put it at eye level directly behind Buster and stuck there with him—or tried to. Every foot of shambling gait, every rise from the rocker, every twist of a move to cat, dog, or parrot, goldfish, door, or window, we had to move with him. Cursing and sweating and wondering why, we shot more 180-degree and 360-degree pans than in a dozen Westerns; the apparently simple little film was not so simple, technically as well as philosophically.

Buster (and almost everybody on the crew) made a few corner-of-the-mouth remarks about his face being his livelihood all these years and here these idiots were knocking themselves out to avoid seeing it. In fact, when even a fraction of profile did get in, as it often did, we immediately did another take, no matter how good the previous one had been. But Keaton's behavior on the set was as steady and cooperative as it had been that first day. He was indefatigable if not exactly loquacious. To all intents and purposes, we were shooting a silent film, and he was in his best form. He encouraged me to give him vocal directions during the shot, sometimes starting over again without stopping the camera if he felt he hadn't done something well the first time. (Nor did he believe much in rehearsal, preferring the spontaneity of performance.) Often when we were stumped over a technical problem with the camera, he came through with suggestions, inevitably prefacing his

Keaton on street location.

The room set. Keaton covering mirror.

comments by explaining that he had solved such problems many times at the Keaton Studios back in 1927, or whenever. He ate lunch with us each day and talked about how differently films were made back then—with no script, starting with an idea about a character in trouble, a series of improvisations and gags to get him out of trouble, finis —but never a direct comment on this one.

About the fourth or fifth day, with the sequence at the window, sidling up in his greatcoat and scarf to pull aside the gauze curtains with his own poetic combination of grace and awkwardness, he caught on that there was more here than had previously met his inner eye. Maybe we had something, and this wasn't just for the dough. He didn't exactly hop up and down, but we could see that he was getting interested.

By the time we got to the sequence with the animals, he was in his element. This was straight slapstick, a running gag, the little man versus a mutely mocking animal world. Mocking, all right. Everyone had told me that dogs were dependable performers and could, with training, do almost anything; cats, on the other hand, tended to be highly erratic and usually wound up as total nuisances. As our menagerie turned out, our huge lump of an alley cat performed splendidly, doing exactly what it was supposed to do; but our dog, a rather shy Chihuahua, started well, if a bit timidly, then froze up completely. On one of the early takes, Buster had been so anxious to get rid of him in order to get back to the cat in time that he dropped him behind the door a bit more unceremoniously than he should have. The dog never recovered his equilibrium, and we lost a fair portion of ours. Nothing was wrong with him physically, but he just didn't trust Buster, or filmmaking.

We spent the better and worse part of a day on that sequence, with lots of laughs from the onlookers but not all of our stuff in the can. Some of the out-takes, with

Keaton and cat.

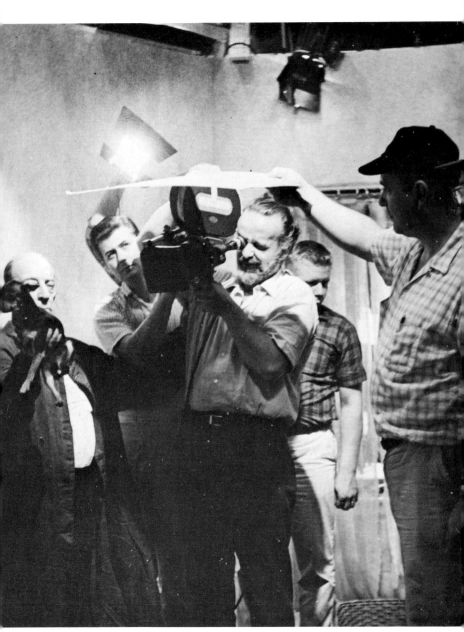

In room set. Keaton with dog, Coffey with camera.

Keaton on street location.

Buster making faces at the animals and breaking up, were funnier than anything in the film. The trouble was that because of the rigid dichotomy of the two visions we couldn't cut anywhere and splice parts of two takes together. Each take had to go on till the end of the shot.

Here again, Buster was patient and understanding, although the Chihuahua didn't think so. So was Sam who, day by day, learned more and more about the curious vicissitudes of making a film. He was always there and always watching from above the set, unobtrusive but dominant, always eager to answer or to look through the camera, or help with a move. I used to look up at him as he sat there for hours, motionless and intent, his elbows akimbo on the light rail, staring down at us through his spectacles like some wise old owl contemplating with interested but detached equanimity a bunch of frantic beavers building some nonsensical mud-stick dam. It must have been very mysterious to him, but at the same time he was rather pleased to be there.

Each day brought new insights and discoveries. After we all began to accept the fact that we were not going to shoot close-ups of Buster's lovely dead-pan visage or have him tap dance to make the script more interesting, the camera-behind-his-back technique grew smoother. Along the way we hit upon some happy accidents. The rocker we were using happened to have two holes in the headrest which began to glare at us. Sam was delighted and encouraged us to include the headrest. The folder from which the photographs were taken had two eyelets, well proportioned. Another pair of "eyes" for O to avoid. We wound up combing the set for more: walls, props, wherever.

We had decided, once the original opening sequence was eliminated, that we would open with a huge menacing close-up of an eye, held as long as possible and then opening to reveal the pupil searching and then focusing—and then

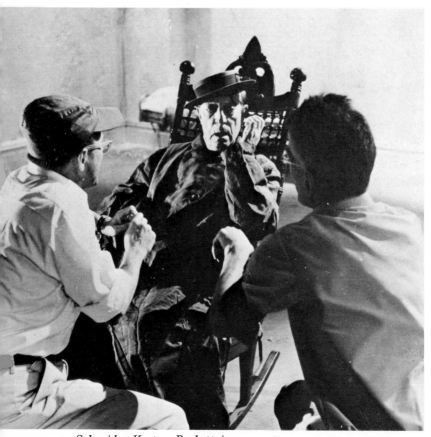

Schneider, Keaton, Beckett, in room set.

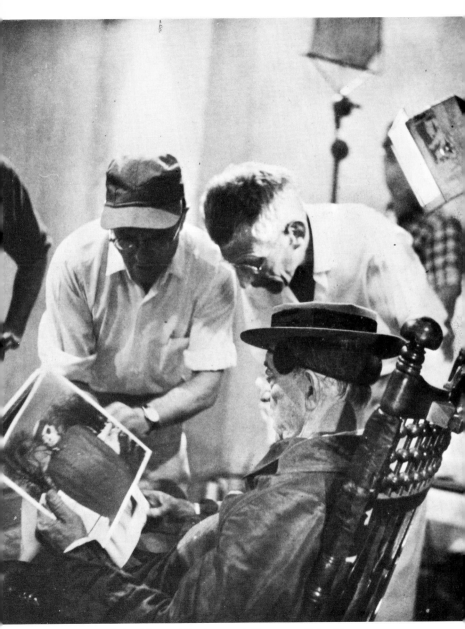

In room set. Schneider and Beckett with Keaton as O looking at photos of Keaton as E.

cut to Keaton running along the wall. The texture of Buster's own eyelid was beautifully creased and reptilian; he was willing to sit for interminable periods of time, with dozens of lamps blazing at him, for us to get several good shots of his eye, open and closed. Ask, and he gave it to us: sitting patiently in his dressing room reading or playing cards, always ready for another take, always somewhat amused by it all, behind his silence.

At last came the day we got not only that (dead) goldfish's eye, but those much more vital final close-ups of Buster's countenance in confrontation with itself. It was or could be a terrifyingly effective last shot, and Buster, finally given his chance not only to let us see his face but to see him act, let loose from deep inside somewhere. When we finally saw it, that face paid off—even if we hadn't known it was Keaton's.

He was surprised, incidentally, that the running time of the film had actually gone past his estimated four minutes. But also pleased. And he knew by the time he was finished with us that it all "meant" something even though he still was not sure exactly what. An actor must not mean but do, he seemed to be saying all along, right up to the hour he left for a train to the West Coast. But whatever he may have subsequently said to interviewers or reporters about not understanding a moment of what he was doing or what the film was about, what I remember best of our final farewell on the set was that he smiled and half-admitted those six pages were worth doing after all.

We had a few inserts and other odds to clear up (without Keaton). But we never did get back to that opening location. Sidney proceeded to do a very quick very rough cut for Sam to look at before taking off for Paris. And that first cut turned out to be not too far off from what we finally had. The editing was painstaking—and painful. Sidney always gently trying to break the mold we had set in

Keaton in room sc

the shooting, and Sam and I in our different ways always gently holding him to it. There was no question of sparring over who had the legal first cut or final cut or whatever. We talked, argued, tried various ways, from moviola to screen and back again, to make it come out as much the film that Sam had first envisioned as we could.

Sometimes I loved it, and sometimes I hated it. Remembering that loss of the opening sequence, and all the things I didn't do or did badly. Feeling that the two-vision thing never worked and that people would be puzzled (they were). Seeing all sorts of technical bloopers that should not have been there. Laughing—and crying—over that bloody Chihuahua and why Buster had to drop him on the first take. (Moral: always have understudies for the animals.) Yet, the film undoubtedly took on an ambience, a strange special snow-soft texture of its own, that gave it depth and richness. Like an abstract painting, or one of Beckett's plays, it grew on you. I was once told that British director Peter Brook had seen it somewhere and had said half of it was a failure and the other half successful. I'm inclined to agree, although I'm not sure we'd both pick the same half.

We had difficulty marketing the film. No one wanted it. No one wants shorts anyhow, and this one they didn't want (or understand) with a vengeance. Nor did showing it around help us. We stopped showing it. It became a lone, very lone, piece indeed. Which no one ever saw, and seemingly very few wanted to see.

Then, in the summer of 1965, came an unexpected offer from the New York Film Festival. Amos Vogel had seen a print somewhere and thought it was worth showing—as part of a Keaton revival series. Already the film was becoming Keaton's and not Beckett's. I fought another losing battle to keep it from getting sandwiched in between two Keaton shorts, a standard one he'd made some years earlier

Beckett in room set.

Keaton and Beckett in room set.

and a new railroad commercial he'd just completed. Both were funny if not great, and they were the expected Keaton. I dreaded what would happen when the unexpected Keaton came on. Then *Film* began—I was practically crouched underneath my balcony seat at the top of Philharmonic Hall (I've never been able to go back there since). The professional film festival audience of critics and students of film-technique started laughing the moment the credits came on, roaring at that lovely grotesque close-up of Buster's eyelid. I could hardly stand it. A moment later they stopped laughing. For good. All through the next twenty-two minutes they sat there, bored, annoyed, baffled, and cheated of the Keaton they had come to see. Who the hell was Beckett? At the end they got up on their hind legs and booed. Lustily. I thought of Godard and Antonioni and a few others at Cannes; wept, and ran.

The critics, naturally, clobbered us or ignored us. One of them called the film "vacuous and pretentious," the exact two things it wasn't, and even told us how stupid we were to keep Keaton's back to the camera until the end. As to the "message"—*esse est percipi*—not one had a clue.

Somehow or other, Sam and I survived (he's absolutely marvelous at doing that; I'm not) and eventually *Film* got shown at various European film festivals, getting lots of coverage and winning several prizes as well as widespread critical interest. Wherever it was shown, sometimes even with other Keaton films, it received respectful attention and at least partial understanding of its intention. Never released generally in this country or abroad, it did have scattered occasional public showings mostly for university audiences, and began to develop what amounted to an underground audience of Beckett or Keaton fans.

Last summer, four years after it was shot, it was finally shown in a New York theater for the general public (in a program of shorts at the Evergreen Theatre) and received

93

generally favorable reviews. Hard as it is for those involved to appreciate each time, that's par for the Beckettian course. All of his stage plays, radio and TV pieces, first get slammed, derided, ignored. Then, five years later, they are hailed as classics.

It's about time for that to be happening to Beckett's *Film*. After all, it's 1969.

—ALAN SCHNEIDER

Hastings-on-Hudson, New York
February, 1969

Production photo credits:
Richard Seaver: 75, 79, 84
Frank Serjack: 62, 64, 69, 70, 80,
            82, 83, 86, 87, 89, 91, 92